#WTFnov8

#WTFnov8

2016 Presidential Election - Self-help us all!

Voters D-Tox Activity Guide & Emergency Kit

Deliberate.Doodle.Describe.Discuss.Demolish.Do!

by Lisa La Bonté

Dedication

To an America that is hurting right now,
I love you.
Get well soon.

ISBN 10: 0-692-79453-1
ISBN 13: 978-0-692-79453-1

Cover and Interior Design by Creative Machinery, Inc.

Van Wagenen Publishing
1101 Wilson Blvd
Arlington, VA 22209

Available from Amazon.com and other retail outlets

This book may also be ordered on our website:
www.wtfnov8.com

Something to Contemplate

The U.S. may not have hit rock bottom, but for many of us, it sure feels like we're close.

No matter the outcome of the 2016 election, in the spirit of positive spin, keep this gem in mind:

"Ruin is a gift. Ruin is the path to transformation."
Elizabeth Gilbert, Author

Acknowledgment

Although this book relates to an American topic of epic proportions, a number of those instrumental in adding inspiration for this book have been following the election from afar and wondering, "WTF is going on in America!? This, let's call it 'fascination', added to the evolution of this book.

Having spent the past decade overseas, I am grateful for my enduring friendships. Alwaleed Abdelrahman and Delila Bencherif, your ideas and experiences were very helpful, thank you!

Special thanks to my Dubai design czar and copyright queen, Rabab, (who shall remain 'family-name'-less as my occasional use of profanity in this book is an embarrassment, I'm certain) love your work ethic and love you lots. Without your patience and talents this book would surely not exist.

To my mother, whose innocent activity idea of "Pin the Tail on the Donkey" proved the spark that ignited two of the book's most irreverent tasks, and whose creative genes I've fortunately inherited.

To my dear friend Zach, thanks for your friendship.

Preface

2016 U.S. Presidential Election Gone Wild

Make no mistake, this is one toxic election cycle. The behavior - past and present - of the leading candidates has created fear, loathing, and enormous levels of stress among a large portion of the American public.

Relationships have eroded, some worse, have imploded. Never in modern history has our society been so torn between two flawed top candidates as the rest of the world looks on, in horror, or perhaps worse, in utter amusement.

This is Serious

This election cycle has seen substantial external interference (accusations of such against kingpins Vladimir Putin and George Soros) and an unprecedented level of media bias and meddling.

The news media has produced an unrelenting daily onslaught of damning fodder against each of the two most undesired candidates perhaps in U.S. history, while social media never sleeps and facilitates, in its reach and sheer message volume, vitriol and hate speech emanating from both sides. Internet allows one to search, anytime, anywhere (critical in this case, as this around-the-clock access further fuels bombardment of stressors that exacerbate feelings of distrust, anger, and even hopelessness). It is quite easy to see how doubt and panic are able to fester. This does not bode well for one's peace of mind now, or the outlook toward the future.

It's apparent that these circumstances are creating an astounding amount of indecision and a resignation as to who deserves a vote November 8th. The inability to decide on an issue of importance in a sound manner or the feeling of "settling", for many, is an enormous source of discomfort and stress.

Further, the U.S. has lost credibility on a number of fronts and it's debatable whether there is a light at the end of this tunnel. How demoralizing! What to do?

Gather your friends or do it solo, either way queue up your scissors, writing utensils, favorite coloring instruments, maybe some glue, and ooh some glitter! Channel you inner child and start flipping through the pages of this book to take your mind off the realities of this bizarre election cycle –if at least for a few moments, here and there.

As the tone of this book is irreverent, you may find content contained within that is not suitable for those under 18 and perhaps even over 18. You've been warned.

As if WTF in the title wasn't enough!
Now, on to election distraction.

How to Use this Activity Book
first, accept that I've made some
core assumptions

- You bought or were given this book. The assumption is that you have some semblance of a sense of humor and adventure –and are having a hell of a time making sense of this election cycle – to put it mildly.

- Concepts like "WTF" don't phase you. That's good, because there are a few risqué activities in this book.

- You don't live your life in 'the box'. You believe – or want to believe – that if properly engaged (ok, distracted), your mind is free to wander in a new direction, no stress, no worry.

- And, speaking of 'wandering', heads up-- there is no Table of Contents. Flipping through this book aimlessly is a good approach. Finding stuff by accident can be fortuitous. Or not.

- I hope that you approach the activities in this book with a similar spirit in which they were created and intended – as irreverent, nostalgic, fun and reflective ways to take your mind off what's in store November 8th and possibly, beyond..

#WTFnov8 attempts to provide some grains of sanity and inspiration along with humor and silliness for cheap therapeutic relief from common election anxiety. (Please, if your situation is more serious, see the back of this book).

This book is organized very simplistically:

and then, there's a
Method to the Madness
Stop

Detox: or for our purposes, D-Tox

DELIBERATE .... **think** about it

DISCUSS .... **talk** about it

DESCRIBE .... **write** about it

DOODLE .... **draw** it

DEMOLISH *(my favorite)* ...... **ruin** to <u>release</u> it!

DATA .... **learn** about it

DO .... **action**!

Each D-Tox activity type is interspersed throughout, in no particular order, and just enough jumbling of topics to keep you engaged (and healthily / hopefully, happily / distracted from this election!).

FREE SPACE FREE SPACE FREE SPACE FREE SPACE FREE SPACE

Free Space

Throughout this book you will see pages with a big "Free Space" badge.

These pages are either the backs (or fronts) of an activity for Demolition or Do-ing or placed there simply for you to jot down ideas or thoughts. Open spaces are for you to fill up with descriptions of your feelings at any given moment in time.

Pass the book around and engage your friends, family, and co-workers.

As you can imagine, this election will be one to remember and this book may serve as a memento of your and your friends' opinions and feelings for years to come.

NEWS FLASH: It's a Thing.

It not only has a name — it has an abbreviation!

It's *Election Stress Disorder (ESD)*, and word has it that **52% of American voters** surveyed by a recent Harris Poll (commissioned by the American Psychological Association) feel a high level of anxiety. Worse, of this figure, an **estimated 71% are suffering from significant stress, or ESD**.

Those most affected include:

Ethnicity   **→ Hispanics**
Age groups **→ New Voters under 21,**
               → Millennials & Seniors

Symptoms include:

- Shattered friendships
- Heightened sense of social divisions
- Hateful missives
- Anger
- Depression ☹
- Feeling of hopelessness

Try to reduce your election anxiety and alleviate your chances of ESD - "DO" this book!

Visit www.apa.org to find out more about ESD

ELECTION STRESS
IN AMERICA

52%
OF U.S.
ADULTS

say the 2016
U.S. presidential
election is a very
or somewhat
significant source
of stress.

59% OF REPUBLICANS | 55% OF DEMOCRATS

Republicans and Democrats are
EQUALLY LIKELY* as one another to
say the election is a very or somewhat
significant source of stress.

*The 4 percentage point difference is considered statistically equivalent.

SOCIAL MEDIA
AND ELECTION STRESS

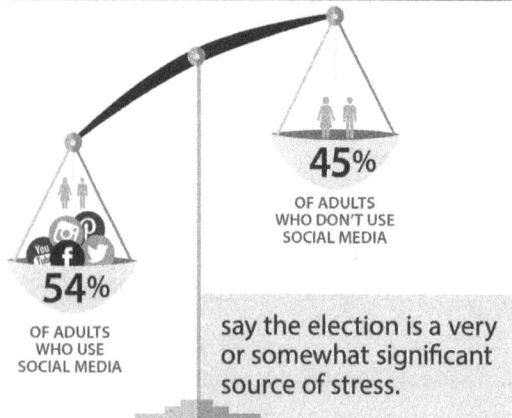

45%
OF ADULTS
WHO DON'T USE
SOCIAL MEDIA

54%
OF ADULTS
WHO USE
SOCIAL MEDIA

say the election is a very
or somewhat significant
source of stress.

The American Psychological Association has suggestions for citizens to aid in managing and potentially reducing stress and anxiety during this election cycle:

- If the 24-hour news cycle of claims and counterclaims from the candidates is causing you stress, limit your media consumption. Read just enough to stay informed. Turn off the newsfeed or take a digital break.

- Take some time for yourself, go for a walk, or spend time with friends and family doing things that you enjoy.

- Avoid getting into discussions about the election if you think they have the potential to escalate to conflict. Be cognizant of the frequency with which you're discussing the election with friends, family members or coworkers.

- Stress and anxiety about what might happen is not productive. Channel your concerns to make a positive difference on issues you care about. Consider volunteering in your community, advocating for an issue you support or joining a local group. Remember that in addition to the presidential election, there are state and local elections taking place in many parts of the country, providing more opportunities for civic involvement.

- Whatever happens on Nov. 8, life will go on. Our political system and the three branches of government mean that we can expect a significant degree of stability immediately after a major transition of government.

- Avoid catastrophizing, and maintain a balanced perspective.

- Find balanced information to learn about all the candidates and issues on your ballot (not just the presidential race), make informed decisions.

- Vote. In a democracy, a citizen's voice does matter. Be sure to wear your "I voted" sticker with pride. By voting, you will hopefully feel you are taking a proactive step and participating in what for many has been a stressful election cycle.

Reprinted with permission from The American Psychological Association's Stress in America survey.
Copyright © 2016, American Psychological Association

I suggest you buy fun and uplifting books, watch comedy series or movies, get outside, get active and get creative! – anything you can do that is constructive is positive reinforcement for your brain and helps you re-direct your thoughts.

Election

Snippets

FREE
SPACE

About the Election & future...

I am registered to vote YES _____ (yay)
NO _____ (boo)

Oh, sorry, no judgment. It's all good

What is/are the biggest issue(s) on your mind for the near future? (1-2 years)

_____

What is/are the biggest issue(s) on your mind for the mid-term future? (3-8 years)

_____

_____

Anything you can do or have done to address these issues?

_____

_____

I identify my political views and positions with a specific party Yes _____ No _____

_____ I plan to Vote & make my voice heard on Nov. 8!
_____ I plan to sit back & hope the outcome is positive!
_____ I've given up all hope!
_____ I am packing and ready to leave the country.

Need to contact your state
Elections Board

URGENTLY?

Pick up the phone!

Beware, some States *REQUIRE 4 WEEKS ADVANCE*
Voter Registration

Alabama: (334) 242-7200
Alaska: (866) 952-8683
Arizona: (877) THE-VOTE
Arkansas: (800) 482-1127
California: (800) 345-8683
Colorado: (303) 894-2200
Connecticut: (860) 509-6100
Delaware: (866) 276-2353
Florida: (850) 245-6200
Georgia: (404) 656-2871
Hawaii: (800) 442-VOTE
Idaho: (208) 334-2852
Illinois: (217) 782-4141
Indiana: (317) 232-3300
Iowa: (515) 281-8849
Kansas: (785) 296-4561
Kentucky: (502) 573-7100
Louisiana: (225) 922-0900
Maine: (207) 624-7736
Maryland: (410) 269-2840
Massachusetts: (617) 727-2828
Michigan: (888) 767-6424
Minnesota: (877) 600-VOTE
Mississippi: (601) 359-6360
Missouri: (573) 751-2301
Montana: (888) 884-VOTE

Nebraska: (888) 727-0007
Nevada: (775) 684-5708
New Hampshire: (603) 271-3242
New Jersey: (609) 292-3760
New Mexico: (505) 827-3600
New York: (518) 474-6220
North Carolina: (919) 733-7173
North Dakota: (701) 328-4146
Ohio: (614) 466-2585
Oklahoma: (405) 521-2391
Oregon: (503) 986-1518
Pennsylvania: (877) 868-3772
Rhode Island: (401) 222-2345
South Carolina: (803) 734-9060
South Dakota: (605) 773-3537
Tennessee: (615) 741-7956
Texas: (800) 252-VOTE
Utah: (877) 9UT-EGOV
Vermont: (802) 828-2464
Virginia: (800) 552-9745
Washington: (800) 448-4881
Washington, DC: (202) 727-2525
West Virginia: (304) 558-6000
Wisconsin: (608) 266-8005
Wyoming: (307) 777-5860

Care to Connect + Share?

We'd love to learn more and hear about your experiences with #WTFnov8 – Send a picture of this page or of a completed #WTFnov8 activity, post with mention to Instagram *@creativemachinery* or Twitter *@ElectionDTox*.

A Follow gets a Follow, a Like or a shared post. Now, tell us more about your state.

1. Family/last name only "THE _____"
2. What's your state's bird? _____
3. What's the slogan on your state's license plate? _____ How many digits?_____
4. Draw your state Flag:

5. Color your flag in (coloring therapy works wonders!)
6. Is your state traditionally "Blue", Blue leaning, "Red", Red leaning, or Purple? _____
7. In which time zone is your state located? ____
8. What's the population of your state? _____
9. What's your state Capital? _____
10. Does it irritate you when someone asks too many questions? Yes ____ No ____

How well do you know your way around your Nation?

Fill in as many States as you can. Color in the ones you've visited ☺

Electoral Votes are allocated based on a state's population.

Can you fill in the number of votes per state?
At least yours?!

Oversimplified
Top Policy Issues 2016

National Security

Issues include critical areas like Defense/ Military, Cybersecurity, Nuclear policy, as well as border control, terrorism, refugee settlement. It's complicated...

Health Care

Issues include the viability of The Affordable Care Act (ObamaCare), who should control healthcare insurance, Medicare, and who decides what treatment choices should be available, and service territories

Immigration Reform

Issues include treatment under the law for illegal immigrants and their children, sanctuary cities, and if stronger immigration controls are needed

Jobs

Unemployment, minimum wage, and pay equity are at issue

Education

Issues include school vouchers, charter schools, standardized testing, governmental controls, and free funding for college

Gun Control

Debate over whether more laws to restrict or regulate gun ownership are needed to reduce gun violence

Reproductive Rights (Abortion)

Debate continues as to whether abortion is a constitutional right and if restrictions should be applied, which ones, also contraceptives policy

Energy & Environment

Issues include pollution control, energy policy, use of federal lands, and considerations and plan about global warming and climate change

Tax Reform

The debate is over whether comprehensive reform of tax code is needed and if personal and corporate tax rates should change, and at what level, for whom

Additionally Important Policies include:

Budget, Social Security, Economy, Free & Fair Trade, Foreign Policy, Crime, Drugs, LGBT Rights, Government Reform, Civil Rights, and more

About this Brief Candidates Overview

The few pages that follow provide a short and sweet mention of the presidential candidate's top policy areas in the fast approaching 2016 election.

As there are more than a dozen core policy issues each with a multitude of sub-policy issues, 'we could be here all day' if we went this route and this would be a very different book.

Further, it's like comparing apples to oranges in many cases, for instance, as one candidate treats Foreign Policy and National Security as one policy issue, another's platform treats Foreign Policy and Defeating ISIS as one issue and National Defense separately. Thus would be unfair to those of you reading this to even attempt to create matrices and determine how to compare candidates accurately. Will leave this to policy wonks (find them online). or your own super sleuthing.

Most vitally, as this book is aimed at stress relief ultimately, I'll pass on dedicating 40 pages to anything more in-depth relating to policy positions, k? I'm doing you a favor, trust me. Deep breath. Good. Let's continue.

Cast of Characters

Top Issues by Candidate
(taken from campaign websites)

Hillary Clinton (Democrat)	Donald Trump (Republican)
<ul><li>Economy & Jobs</li><li>Education</li><li>Environment</li><li>Health</li><li>Justice & Equality</li><li>National Security</li></ul>	<ul><li>Constitution & Second Amend.</li><li>Cybersecurity</li><li>Economy</li><li>Education</li><li>Energy</li><li>Foreign Policy & Defeating ISIS</li><li>Healthcare</li><li>Immigration</li><li>Tax Plan</li><li>Trade</li><li>Veterans Affairs Reform</li><li>National Defense</li><li>Regulations</li><li>Childcare</li></ul>
6 categories with many sub-category descriptions on her website	*14 categories, in-depth on his website*

Top Issues by Candidate
(taken from campaign websites)

Gary Johnson (Libertarian)	**Jill Stein** (Green)
<ul><li>Wasteful spending</li><li>Taxes</li><li>Term Limits</li><li>Jobs</li><li>Civil Liberties</li><li>Foreign Policy & National Defense</li><li>Religious Freedom & Non-Discrimination</li><li>Supporting Veterans</li></ul>	<ul><li>Climate Action</li><li>Jobs as a Right</li><li>End Poverty</li><li>Education as a Right</li><li>Healthcare as a Right</li><li>A Just Economy</li><li>Freedom & Equality</li><li>Criminal Justice Reforms</li></ul>
15 categories, overviews on his website	*16 categories with details on her website*

www.johnsonweld.com   www.jill2016.com

Check out **Evan McMullin,** Independent candidate on ballot in
11 states: **www.evanmcmullin.com**

BIG PART

of mental well-being
includes feeling good about
your decisions and actions

YOUR VOTE *IS*

YOUR VOICE

IS

YOUR
CHOICE

MAKE IT COUNT!
Do it Well & Do it often

(oops, strike that last part)!
Tuesday, Nov. 8

Super Sites* to Help Make Sense of 2016 Nonsense!

Interactive quiz to find out how your beliefs match each political party. Site available in many languages

www.isidewith.com

Non-partisan (unbiased) in-depth candidate and election information

www.votesmart.org

Compare positions between candidates on 75 issues

www.2016election.procon.com

Where each of the 2016 candidates stand on the issues

www.ontheissues.org

Election and campaign contributions, PACs, SuperPACs, and more

www.opensecrets.org

These are my faves –I'd love to learn about more, so email me yours! Info@wtfnov8.com

American voters

337 million Total U.S. Population
225 million # Possible voters (18 or over)
136 million # Voters in 2008 election
128 million # Voters in 2012 election

2016 ????!!!!!

$19,720,829,751, 221

Amount of USA's national debt (trillions) as of Oct. 15, 2016 (add $ for every elapsed second)

EACH citizen (even kids) currently owes $64,909 as their share of the public debt. And you thought student debt was bad..

$45,486 of debt per SECOND!

TOP 5 ISSUES FOR MILLENNIALS

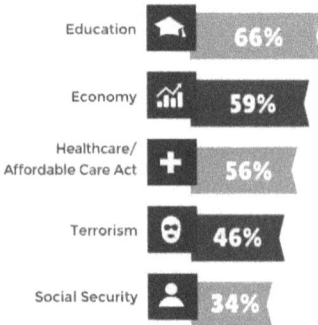

Issue	%
Education	66%
Economy	59%
Healthcare/ Affordable Care Act	56%
Terrorism	46%
Social Security	34%

PERCEPTIONS OF POLITICAL SYSTEM

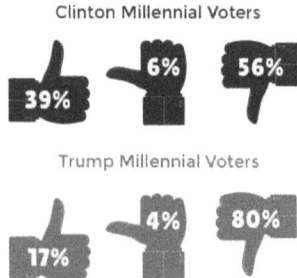

Clinton Millennial Voters
39% 6% 56%

Trump Millennial Voters
17% 4% 80%

Source: Millennials Presidential Election Study in partnership with Millennials Paving Way Series, 2016

Infographics by Millennial Mix (MMX) & Paradigm Sample - 2016

POLITICIANS & PUBLIC SERVANTS

in OUR GOVERNMENT at EVERY level
WORK FOR | THE PEEPS | (US!)

NOT the other way around.

Me thinks they need reminding...

make your voice heard
on social media using
#WeThePeeps
if you agree

Much Debate but In a Nutshell

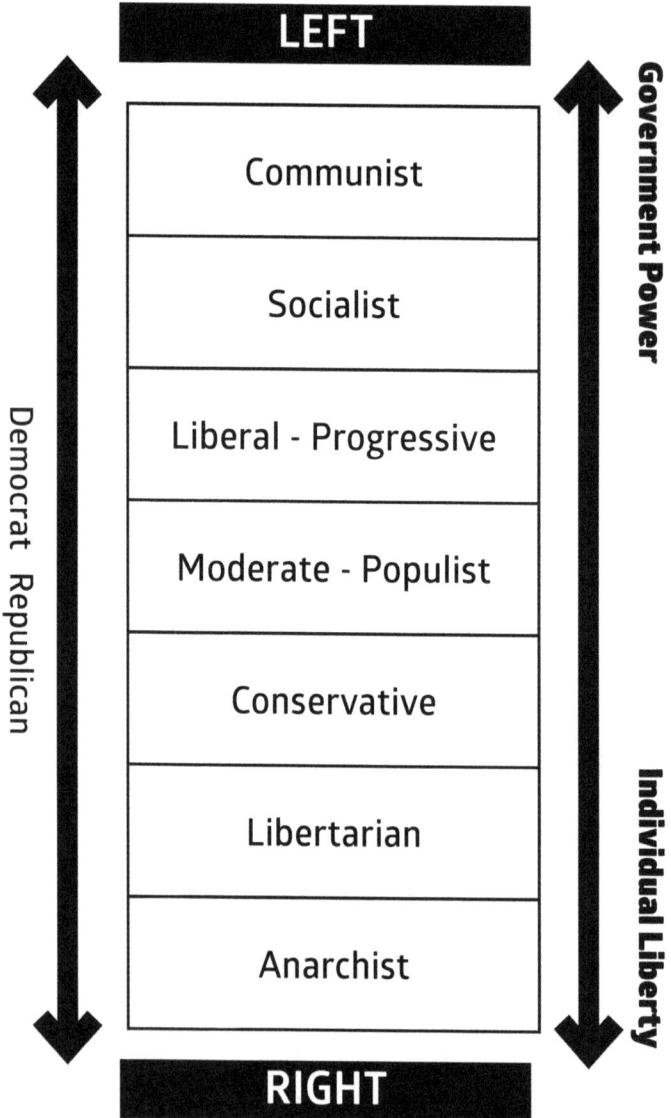

LEFT

Government Power

Communist

Socialist

Liberal - Progressive

Moderate - Populist

Conservative

Libertarian

Anarchist

Democrat Republican

Individual Liberty

RIGHT

KEEP
CALM
AND
CAST YOUR
VOTE!

R.I.P. Candidacy of
Bernie Sanders for President

A moment of silence, please. Have your friends, family, strangers, and dog, add their messages of condolence here.

Create a Ransom Note for a Hijacked Election

[Glue the letters cut from newspapers or magazines like you see in crime dramas]

After, check out www.ransomizer.com/

Purging is cleansing

Before we get rolling and on to the creative stuff, let's get a sense of the issues irking, upsetting, baffling, intriguing, and otherwise stressing you out.

What are some of the reasons the 2016 election is on your mind. *(Going to try to get these reasons OFF your mind in the next 125 pages).*

**Release any negativity!
Doodle Un-words to describe
this election.**

Un-

Un-

Un-impressive

Un-

Un-

Un-

Un-desirable

Un-

Un-

Un-

New word: **Un-presidented!**

SOMETIMES WE JUST NEED A LITTLE **ATTITUDE** ADJUSTMENT.

A little **tweak** here, a little **shot** of somethin' there..

Decisions... decisions...

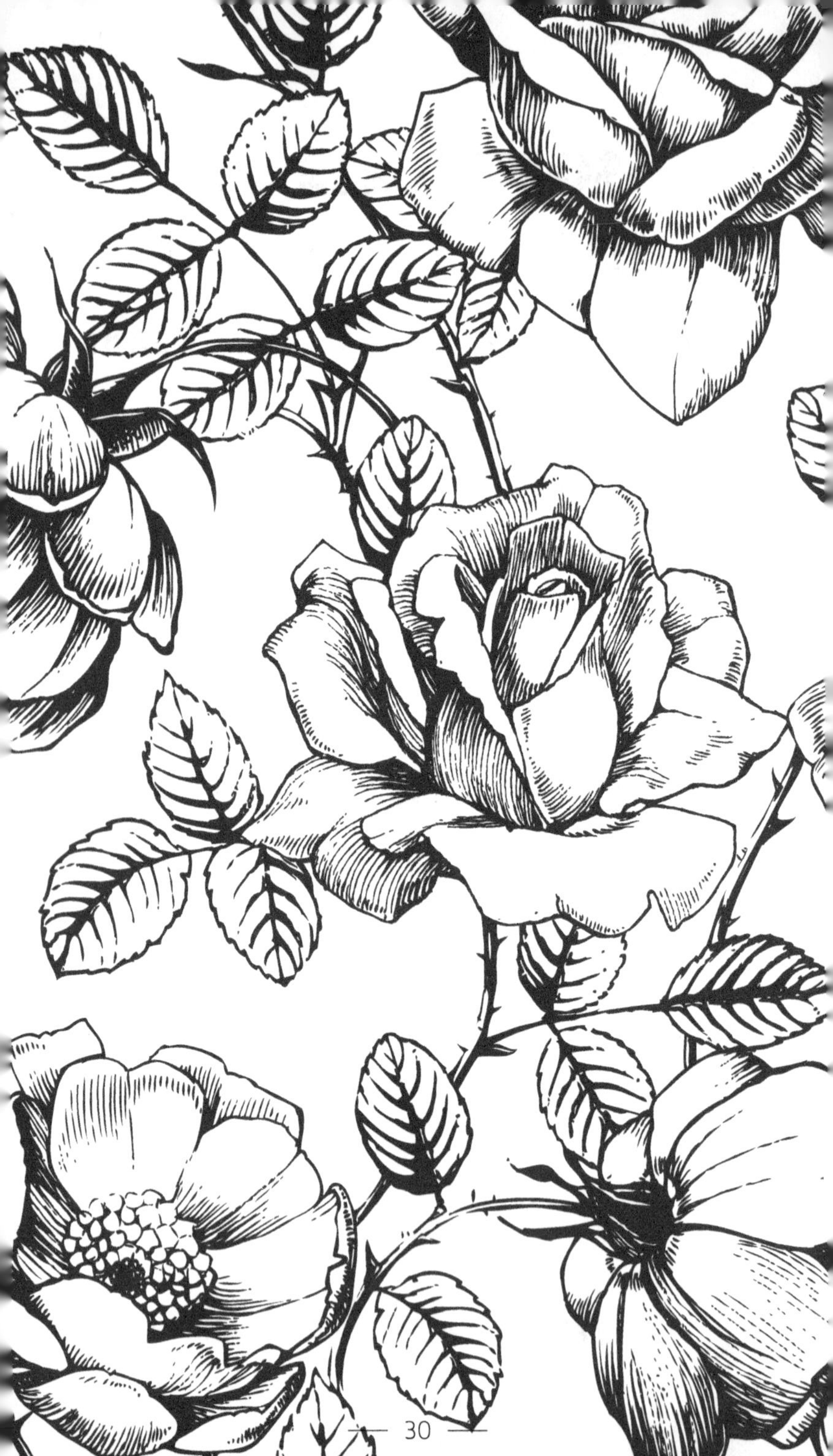

Tear out this page

Run it over with a car. (Ask a bus driver to do it, better)

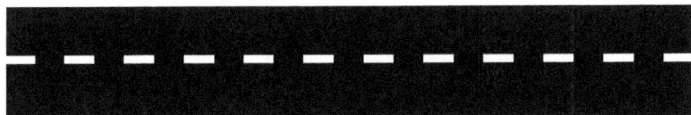

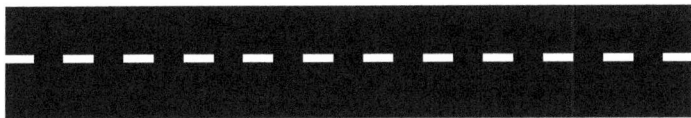

Put it back in the book or in any random place.

Repeat after me, out loud:

I love my friends

Call one if you're in need of a pick-me-up. Social relationships do wonders for warding off depression. And, this election is a total downer. Friend up.

No time to travel?

Color your mood while creating a story in your head of all the things you'd do if you could, in the location that contains these landmarks.

My travel wish list includes:

_____

_____

Consider How Realistic your Frustrations or Fears

about the opposite candidate of choice winning the election.

Issues   *Current Outlook*   *The Likely Outcome*

What is the first thing that comes to mind when you see this?

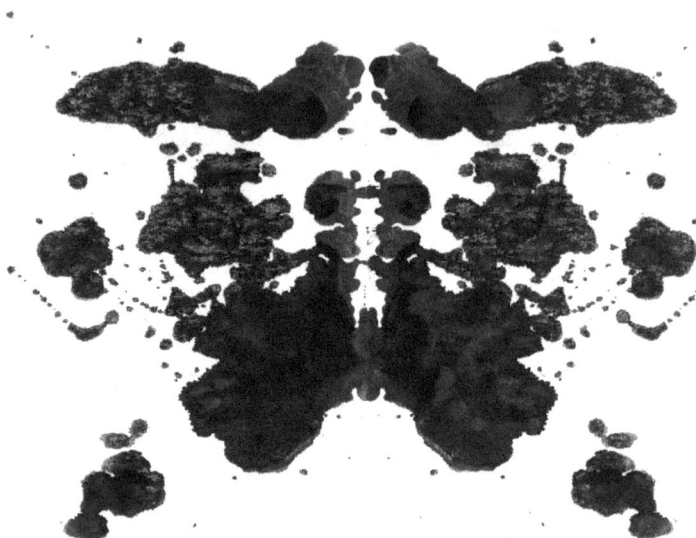

Disclaimer: you may need professional help. ask your mother.

Draw
2 Donkeys

Now, find one to autograph this page.

Do you notice anything?

A. Hillary's Pinocchio nose

B. Donald's .... (ok...., I switched it out)

C. Washington Monument

D. I see a pattern.

Look around you and see if you can find any more examples of phallic symbols. List:

Start a trend if bored
#PHALLICsymbols

CRUMPLE IT
INTO A BALL
AND ***THROW*** IT
AT THE <u>FIRST</u>
PERSON YOU SEE
WITH

ORANGE HAIR

FREE
SPACE

Decompress, Detach, Unplug

Switch off or silence your phones

Avoid checking social media feeds and status updates

Try it a little bit each day until soon it becomes a healthy habit

Note: I realize this is a tough habit to create. Take baby steps.
Cold turkey is best the day after Thanksgiving :p

Be Creative With Your Money

Can you name 3 US States that contain the Letter "B"

1. ~~~~~~~~~~~

2. ~~~~~~~~~~~

3. _____ ?

Re-imagine and draw the other half

Repeat Out Loud:

And, pray realllly hard that this is the case for your chosen candidate!

Act out a Soap Opera Scene – better yet, Opera!

Choose. Set the scene, create your script, and Action! Act out with a friend also in need of election distraction. (If you recall this scene below, reward yourself later for your cultural sophistication) ☺

Use this example, pretend you're Auditioning for role:

A drawing-room in a Vienna hotel, richly appointed and newly furnished in the style of the 1860's. Adelaide is seated at a table, opposite the fortune-teller, Zdenka, in boy's clothes, is seated at another table, busy with all kinds of papers

FORUNE-TELLER
The cards are more auspicious than they were last week.

ADELAIDE
I hope they are.
There is a knock at the door.
We cannot be disturbed.

ZDENKA
(answers the knock; somebody hands her a letter at the door)

ADELAIDE
(shaking her head)
Not now! Put it down there.

ZDENKA
At least it will have company!

ADELAIDE
Still, child. What do the cards say? Tell me! I'm so upset and worried I can't sleep at night.

...

Seek out the rest, it's superb!
Eternal thanks to Richard Strauss

Focus this page on the Nation's capital, also called The Capitol & Doodle D.C. like A Boss

Create your own irreverent Bumper Stickers:

Practice fairness and create <u>1 IN FAVOR</u> of **Hillary Clinton**, <u>1 AGAINST, (or, two that could go either way!)</u> Samples that already exist:

Color yours in when done!

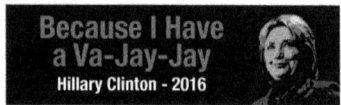

Grab your Blankie & some crayons, it's COLORING TIME!

Drawing created by German Illustrator Bobsmade. Get inspired at www.bobsmade.com

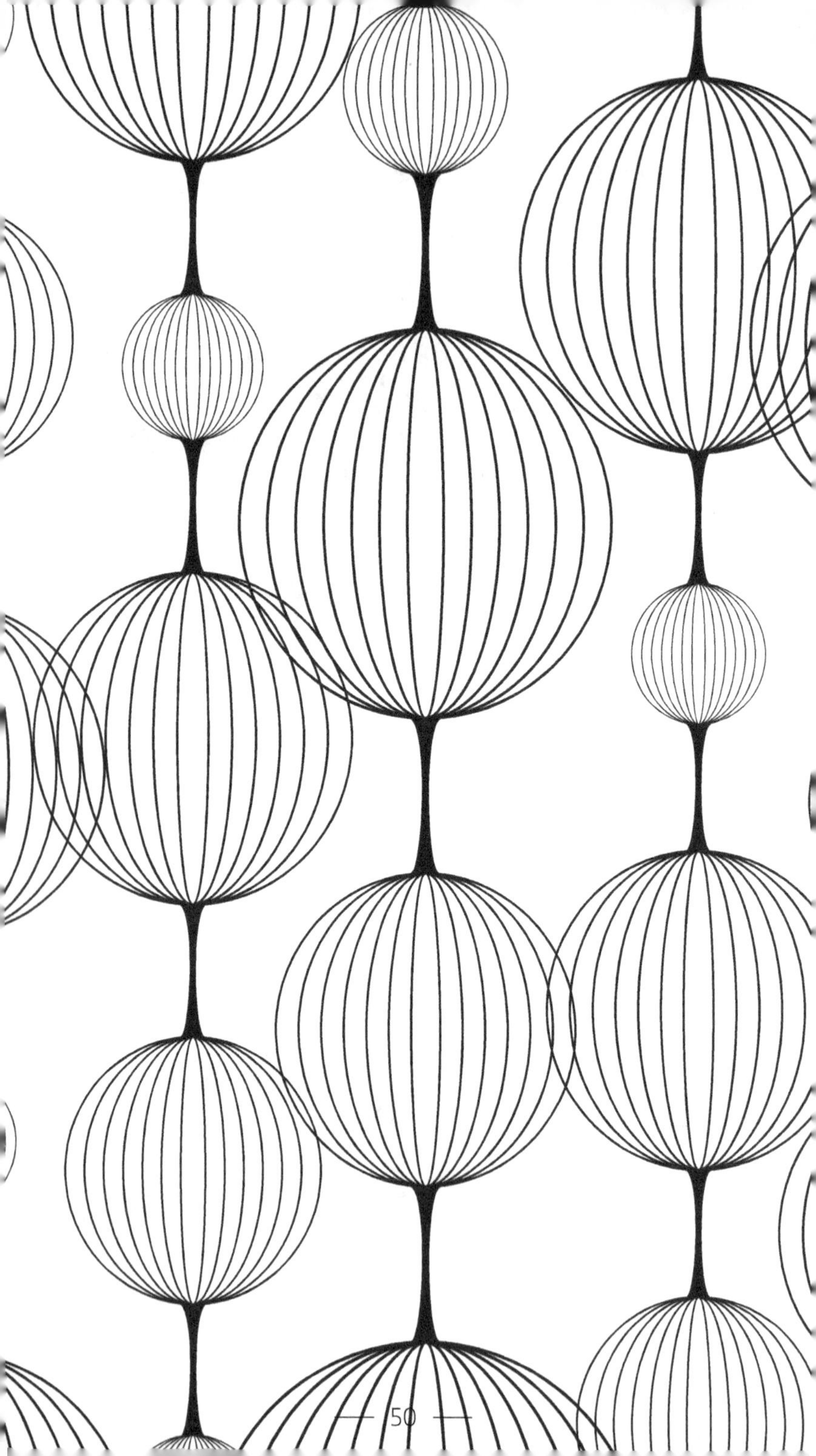

Dance!

LIKE THERE IS NO HIDDEN CAMERA RECORDING YOUR EVERY HOT MOVE

THE
DONALD
FOR PRESIDENT
TRUMP/PENCE

1. Color in if you are feeling optimistic!

2. Cut out and pin to your shirt.

3. Parade around your office or campus and time/count how long it takes to get:

- 3 sneers
- 3 eye-rolls
- 3 snide remarks

Write this number down on any part of page that remains.

FREE SPACE

Word Dump

Add your one or two word descriptions relating to the things that have you stressed out about this damn election cycle.

Staple a perfectly good
$1 dollar bill here

Wait for 2 years and see how much it's worth
if the wrong candidate is elected and economy
goes to shit. In 2019, carefully detach it, as you
may need it.

Keep Some Devilish Stuff Out
of the White House in January.
Color in the meantime.

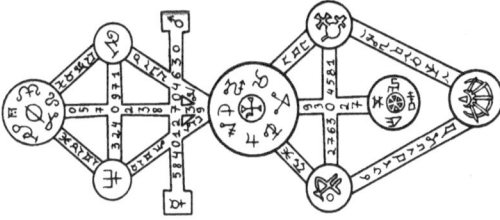

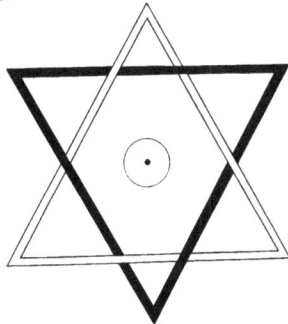

Today is _____

Dear Diary,

_____

_____

_____

_____

_____

_____

_____

_____

_____

Cheer Up with Summer at The Beach or...Plan B:

✿🌾 Doodle hammocks by the sea 🌾✿

LIQUID LIFE

Did you know? Dehydration can cause headaches, poor digestive function, and... bitchiness? Water keeps you human --and alive. Cheers!

FREE SPACE

~~Cucumber~~ Donald
Pin the ~~Tail~~ on The ~~Donkey~~

You will need:

- 2 or more players
- Some wall space
- Scissors
- Tape
- 1 blindfold (eyemask, tie, scarf)

1. Tear the next page (Donald) out and tape to the wall.

2. Determine the size you will use for Donald's cucumber (the cleanest it's gonna get, folks)

3. Cut out a 'penis' (or, make your own, we don't wanna know about it). Replicate for total number of players

4. Each player gets one (put a piece of tape on each)

5. Take turns. Blindfolded, hold your cutout 'cucumber' as others spin you around 5 times.

6. Attempt to walk toward correct wall and tape the cucumber on The Donald.

7. When done, remove blindfold and check your accuracy. Give the next person the chance.

8. The one who comes closest to target, wins

Tear out and tape on a wall

Don't FORGET to BE awesome

YEAR BOOK
STYLE

Pass around for friends to sign

WTF! ELECTION
Pre-nov8

Print & paste favorite
picture of yourself

Pass around for friends to sign

WTF! ELECTION
Post-nov8

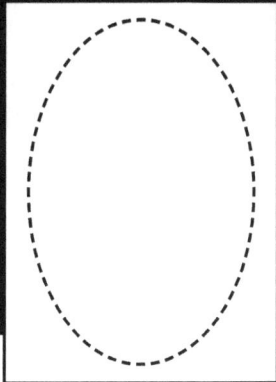

Print & paste picture
of your face after the
outcome of election is
announced

Time for a break & some Music therapy!

1. find a favorite tune on your phone or download one

2. blast the volume

3. belt that puppy out like no one attractive is listening

Singing out loud is a great way to alleviate stress and feel happy at the same time.

Stress Destruction

Take your frustration, aggression, irritation...
out on this PAGE.

TEAR IT OUT !!

RIP *it into* SHREDS

A. While letting out your best version of diabolical laugh

B. In front of perfect strangers for shock value

C. To prove to an unsuspecting family member that you are REALLY MAD about this election (& A BADASS)

How many pieces can you rip it into? Record so far is 115. Certainly you can do better?

P.S. Put litter in it's place.

FREE SPACE

Drink to Forget

Pour yourself and your friends (21 yrs. or over, far, far away from machinery or motor vehicles) very large glasses of something wet and uplifting.

For every 4 minutes that no one mentions politics or the election, everyone takes a swig, shot, sip, whatever.

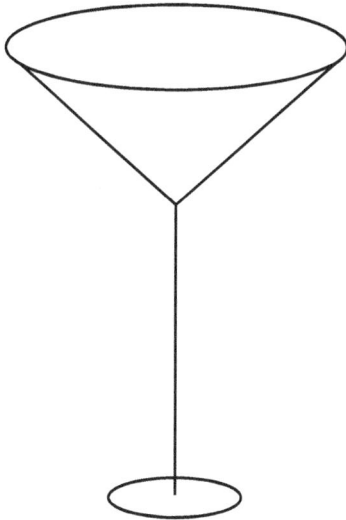

(After 5 hours, if still coherent, consider yourselves cured. Until tomorrow's news cycle...)

Draw
16 Elephants

Now, find one to autograph this page.

Yum!

Time Out!

What size shoe do you wear?

How many presidential elections have you voted in?

REMEMBER

How old you were when you lost your first tooth?

What nickname do you call your mother?

How often do you CALL your mother?

What day is it today?

What time did you wake up? _____

How much do you weigh? Bit personal? Okay, forget it.

What color is your car?

No car? How do you get to work?

No work? What's your hobby?

Ask your Boss a question here that they'll never see and that you've wondered about

_____
_____

What are you thinking about right now?

Color and Doodle around me,
BIGLEAGUE (bigly!)

Go to the best soundproof place you can find
(a car, a closet, a deserted forest).
Yell at the top of your lungs:

F*CK this Election!

F*CK!!

Do you feel better? Repeat as necessary for
unconventional stress release.

<u>Note</u>: "Fuck" is the best emphatic (and
versatile) word, ever! Studies have shown
swearing relieves stress.
*If you are one who cannot stomach the sound of
this word, TEAR THIS PAGE OUT! At which point, bet
you'll feel better!*

FREE SPACE

THINK FAST!

WHEN WAS THE LAST
TIME YOU PLAYED

HOOKY?

DON'T RECALL?
YOU ARE OVERDUE!

Celebrate the
Magical Healing Powers of...

"*There is nothing better than a friend, unless it is a friend with **chocolate**.*" ~**Linda Grayson**

"*Without pain, how could we know joy?' This is an old argument in the field of thinking about suffering and it's stupidity and lack of sophistication could be plumbed for centuries but suffice it to say that the existence of broccoli does not, in any way, affect the taste of **chocolate**.*" ~**John Green, The Fault in Our Stars**

"*Strength is the capacity to break a **Hershey** bar into four pieces with your bare hands - and then eat just one of the pieces.*" ~**Judith Viorst, Love & Guilt & The Meaning Of Life, Etc**

Viva La France! "*He showed the words "**chocolate** cake" to a group of Americans and recorded their word associations. "Guilt" was the top response. If that strikes as unexceptional, consider the response of French eaters to the same prompt: "celebration.""*~**Michael Pollan, In Defense of Food: An Eater's Manifesto**

"*All you need is love. But a little **chocolate** now and then doesn't hurt.*" ~**Charles M. Schulz**

Conduct original SMILE ☺ research

Be brave. Smile at the first 20 people you see today.

How many smiled back?

Do not be concerned about those who didn't (it happens). Rather than feel bad, CHOOSE to feel GOOD! ☺ ☺ You made a positive effort. Awesome. Make it a habit.

Exercise Much?

No nagging.

No judgments.

just
...consider it

it's proven to be uplifting to the spirit (not to mention your hiney)

Mini **SLAMBOOK**

Waaat? How does this work, you ask?

Slambooks started years ago as a schoolyard activity and were a cross between passing notes in class and a private journal. This old-fashioned method was the way friends would gain insights about each other and trends, and, well, okay, gossip perhaps. See if you can keep this positive and uplifting for election distraction + de-stress!

First create a Master page of #s and Names and then move on to the first meaty page by asking a probing question as to opinions, ideas, plans, etc. You want to ask a Q that can be answered in a few words. Example could be, "What quality do you like best about the candidate of your choosing?" or "If you had the chance for a Presidential Appointment, in which governmental department would you like to work?"

Once you're ready to introduce to your inner circle, you may need to explain the concept a bit. Part of the fun of a Slambook is reading others' comments. At least this was fun in the "old days"! ;p And,,, you may be an expert at this and welcome its return. If not, try it as part of an American historical experience!

I'll ask another question on next page to get your Slambook started and then answer it as one of your (new) friends!

Master Name sheet

friends, family, and coworkers can sign up on any # below

Now give them the book so they can answer Q's on next pages using their chosen number

1.

2.

3.

4.

5. Lisa La Bonté

6.

7.

8.

9.

10.

Q1: Your candidate won! yay! In which nation would you like your Ambassadorship?

1.

2.

3.

4.

5. Norway

6.

7.

8.

9.

10.

Q2: _____

_____

_____

1.

2.

3.

4.

5. ?!

6.

7.

8.

9.

10.

Q3: _____

_____

_____

1.

2.

3.

4.

5. ?!

6.

7.

8.

9.

10.

Put Future Possibilities in Focus

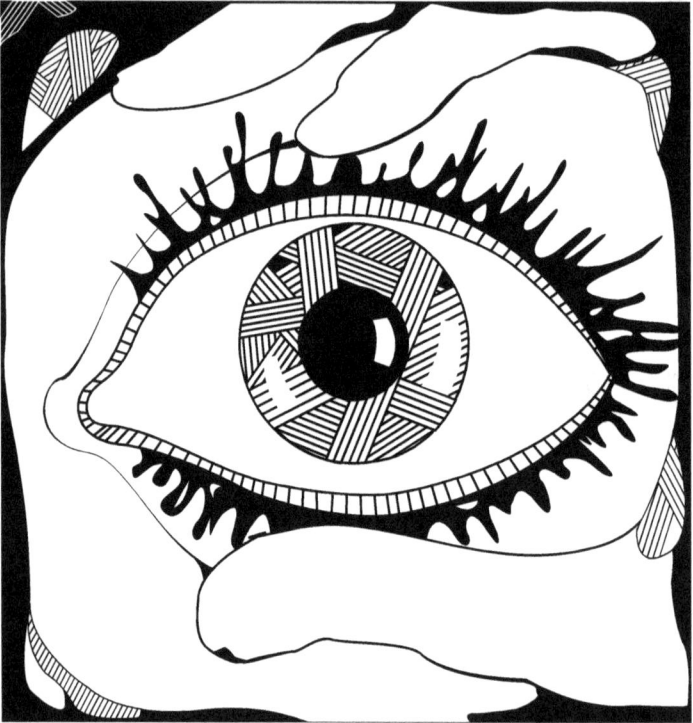

No matter who wins, life goes on, as good as
YOU make it!

You want answers?
Electoral Votes per U.S. State

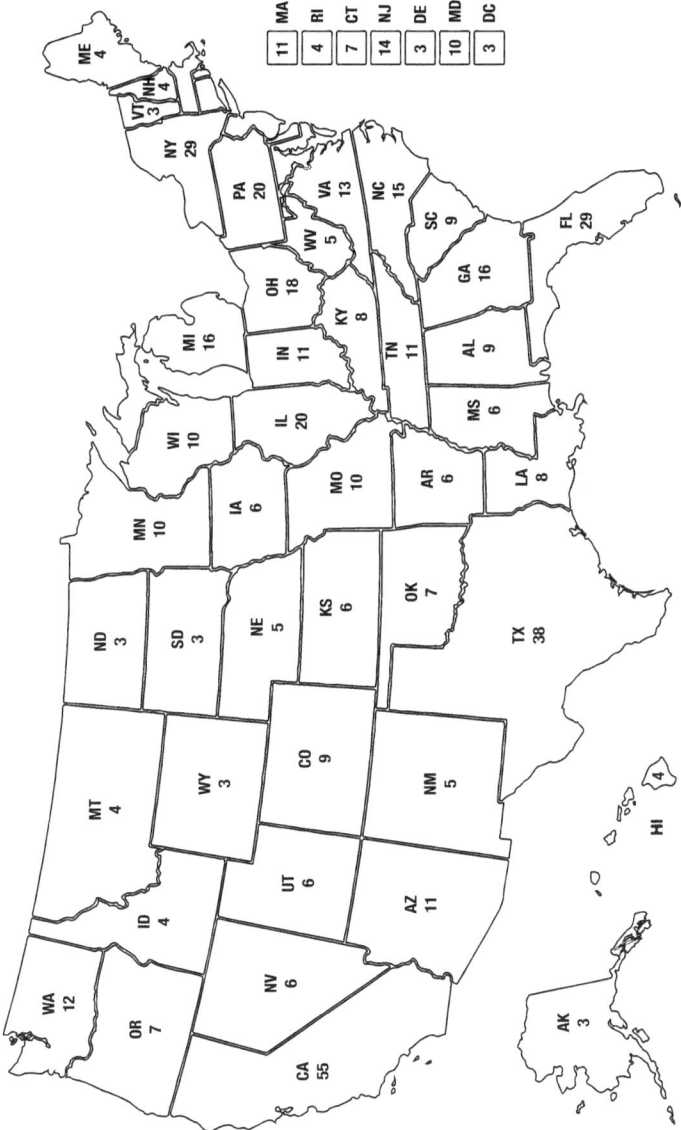

MA	RI	CT	NJ	DE	MD	DC
11	4	7	14	3	10	3

ME 4

VT 3 / NH 4

NY 29

PA 20

VA 13

NC 15

SC 9

FL 29

WV 5

GA 16

OH 18

KY 8

MI 16

IN 11

TN 11

AL 9

IL 20

MS 6

WI 10

MO 10

AR 6

LA 8

IA 6

MN 10

OK 7

ND 3

SD 3

NE 5

KS 6

TX 38

CO 9

NM 5

MT 4

WY 3

HI 4

UT 6

AZ 11

ID 4

WA 12

OR 7

NV 6

AK 3

CA 55

SOME U.S. STATES REQUIRE 3 OR MORE WEEKS <u>ADVANCE REGISTRATION</u> TO EXERCISE YOUR RIGHT TO **VOTE**!

OMG!!!

It's the age of technological advancement **& INSTANT GRATIFICATION**

THE NOW GENERATION

FOR THE LOVE OF GOD, "ELECTION REFORM"!

DOODLE

your cares away here

Donald J. Trump

In your most creative state using different color crayons, write down only nice and pleasant words that start with "J".

I know. Bummer, Jentleman doesn't really start with J.

Get Engaged in the Community – Give back. See how that feels

- Go to a place of worship with a grandparent and meet their friends

- Visit a retirement home, listen to great stories.

- Donate to a local crowd funding project. (There are now over 2,000 sites globally to choose from)

- Donate to any charity, here are some I think are special:
    - Shriners Hospital
    - St. Jude (for Children)
    - ASPCA
    - American Cancer Society
    - Boys & Girls Club
    - YMCA
    - American Heart Assoc.

Find charities :

LIST OF CHARITIES BY AREA:
http://greatnonprofits.org

RATINGS:
www.charitywatch.org
http://www.consumerreports.org
(search 'charities')

FREE
SPACE

Pinocchio Nose ~~Pin the Tail on The Donkey~~ Hillary

[Blast from the Past - Birthday Party Dizziness]

You will need:

- Scissors
- 2 or more players
- Some wall space
- Tape
- 1 blindfold (eyemask, tie, scarf, ?)

1. Tear the next page (Hillary) out and tape to the wall.
2. Cut out the 'nose' below and using other paper replicate for total number of players
3. Each player gets one (put a piece of tape on each)
4. Take turns. Blindfolded, hold your cutout 'nose' as others spin you around 5 times.
5. Attempt to walk toward correct wall and tape the 'nose' on the Hillary.
6. When done, remove blindfold and check your accuracy. Give the next person the chance.
7. The one who comes closest, wins

Tear out and tape on a wall

FREE SPACE

Cultivate Positive Emotions
(negative ones are bah humbug)

○ Choose a relatively quiet location and look up at the sky. Ponder its expansiveness. Consider all that's good in your life.

○ Make yourself a picnic lunch and go to your favorite spot with a friend.

○ Buy a green plant - if you can commit to watering it regularly (dead plants don't cultivate positive emotions).

○ Buy some flowers. Take a big whiff.

○ Better yet, pick some flowers (just not from your neighbors yard).

○ Push any negative emotions OUT of your mind as soon as they enter.

○ Write down and rehearse positive messages (affirmations), Recite to yourself daily.

○ Look in the mirror and smile big as you say "I'm awesome!"

○ There is no reason the glass can't be more than half full. The glass is MORE THAN half FULL! Trust yourself. Embrace optimism.

○ Create a garden and watch it come to life and grow.

Get your coloring groove on

Name 10 things that give you a feeling of

Bliss

Feeling Bogged Down?

FLOSS!
(and then brush with great smelling toothpaste)

insert some teeth

Not only will you feel lighter immediately and have better breath,

flossing is good for your heart and studies suggest this can add years to your life.

(Look it up!)

Maybe you'll even make some new friends!

1. Tear out as much of this page as you feel like at this moment.

2. Spit on it or deface it in some other way that includes bodily fluids (Note: DNA will be exposed so guard this page with your life)

3. Let dry.

4. Attach it back into the book anyway you can and anywhere you feel is a good fit.
...or smash it with a hammer or "bleach"

FREE
SPACE

Inhale

DO A BREATHING EXERCISE OF YOUR CHOICE

Exhale....Ahh...

Repeat...Lighten up ☺

Live Aloha

Deliberate on that.

DID YOU KNOW?

There is a
9%↑ increase*
in **STRESS LEVEL** for
those who use

SOCIAL MEDIA!

Doesn't take much pondering to figure out why.

Tip:

Use the Golden Rule of "Do Unto Others as You Would Have Them Do Unto You" in your posts & let's get a smidge closer to World Peace

*www.apa.org Harris Poll survey Oct. 2016

Do whatever the hell you want on this page. Whatever you do, try to make it positive

Today is _____

Dear Diary,

_____

_____

_____

_____

_____

_____

_____

_____

_____

FREE SPACE

Dip your knuckles in something

MESSY

make an imprint here

more! DOODLE Therapy

Draw the new president on January 21 sitting at their desk in the Oval office.

Add More ☀ to Your Life!

Sunshine is used by our bodies to create ***Vitamin D*** which provides **health benefits** that may help ward off serious illnesses such as cancer, heart disease, and more --including mental benefits such as a boosted mood!

You can become more optimistic, positive and cheerful just by getting a little sun!

Proven Mood Boosters

- Volunteer at a start-up company

- Spend down time making a collage of favorite photos (physical, paper based photos, remember those?!). Display so you see happy memories every day.

- Create a "Treasure Map". Cut out words, pictures, and other items that project a future you. Your mind will help you work toward becoming or attaining it –and you won't even 'know' it!

- Think about all you're grateful for and make a cheat sheet you can keep handy.

- Write a letter to yourself of the future about how you're feeling right now. Hide in a place where you'll find it one day.

- Meditate or practice Yoga, Tai chi or even Feng shui!...

- Re-arrange or decorate your bedroom.

Re-imagine and draw the other half

COLOR YOUR DEPLORABLE HEART OUT AFTER 🖤

Drink to Distract

(ages <21 & those who prefer being sober)

Pour yourself and friend(s) an exotic, healthy, or comforting beverage. Try pomegranate juice or perhaps a mocha machiato.

For every 2 minutes you don't speak of the election, politics, or generally anything toxic, reward with sips all around.

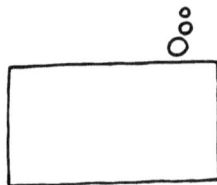

No idea the rest of this activity, so just make it up as you go along.

International much?

QUICK! In 60 seconds, name 10 nations that do NOT **contain the Letter "A". Okay, take another 5 minutes.**

_____

_____

_____

_____

_____

_____

_____

_____

List 8 synonyms for YUGE!
backwards:

enormous = __SUOMRONE__

= _____

= _____

= _____

= _____

= _____

= _____

= _____

= _____

Put your pet's paw print here

DO
NOT
DOODLE ON
THIS PAGE
WHILE DRIVING.

Otherwise, draw a picture of a new toy you'll buy with your next paycheck as a reward for surviving the election thus far.

Furry Companions (aka pets)

If you're feeling a bit 'incomplete' and you otherwise have positive relationships with humans (and the aliens among us), yet have no outlet for all your love and attention or your home is just too quiet, you might VERY carefully consider adopting a (rescue ☺) animal as a pet.

(Notice I didn't write "if you're feeling bored" or "if you're prone to impetuous decisions")

And, if you're not quite sure and want to give pet parenthood a try without any negative effects on the 'little guy', consider "fostering" an animal SHORT term ☺

If you can plan to commit part of your life for the next 10 -20 years (God willing more, not less) to a new member of the family (who won't argue, and is a great listener) you will find this likely a fantastic decision and long term attitude enhancer.

A PLEA: ...As LOVELY as pets can be for your well-being and positivity, they are A TON OF WORK and require actual (sometimes, near constant) attention. Especially "puppy–cats" and large parrots... So be sure you can commit because they deserve to be happy too.

And... **when all else fails in your efforts at pre- or post- election stress...**

REMEMBER!

There are always those tried and true outlets of shopping & ice cream

Remind yourself of your favorite shops

_____

_____

_____

_____

_____

& favorite flavors

_____

_____

_____

_____

_____

FREE SPACE

Create your own irreverent Bumper Stickers:

Practice fairness and create <u>1 IN FAVOR</u> of **Donald Trump**, <u>1 AGAINST, (or, that could go either way!)</u> Samples that already exist:

DEPORT TRUMP

Time to get tough
ELECT TRUMP

Color yours in when done!

Good
food

Good
mood

If you are **feeling *deeply depressed***, or ***worse***, ***having feelings of suicide***, or if you are in need of an anonymous, free ear to express you thoughts and feelings, reach out below. PLEASE, this is a personal request, PLEASE reach out if you are in need.

You are not alone and help is available

Youth & Teen Hotlines
National Youth Crisis Support:
1-800-448-4663

National Adolescent Suicide Helpline:
1-800-621-4000

Youth America Hotline:
1-877-YOUTHLINE (1-877-968-8454)

Covenant House Nine-Line (Teens):
1-800-999-9999

Boys Town National:
1-800-448-3000

Teen Helpline:
1-800-400-0900

TeenLine:
1-800-522-8336

Youth Crisis Support:
1-800-448-4663 **or** 1-800-422-0009

Suicide Hotline

Suicide Hotline:
1-800-SUICIDE (2433)

Suicide & Depression Crisis Line:
1-800-999-9999

National Suicide Prevention Helpline:
1-800-273-TALK (8255)

NDMDA Depression Hotline – Support Group:
1-800-826-3632

Veterans:
1-877-VET2VET

Crisis Help Line – For Any Kind of Crisis:
1-800-233-4357

Additional Support

Panic Disorder Information and Support:
1-800-64-PANIC (1-800-647-2642)

Parental Stress Hotline:
1-800-632-8188

Help Finding a Therapist:
1-800-THERAPIST (1-800-843-7274)

Alcoholics Anonymous:
1 212-870-3400 www.aa.org

Drug Treatment & Hotline:
Substance Abuse & Mental Health Services Administration
1-800-662-HELP (4357)

Thanks to Dana Zarcone

Always Thankful for True Friends

Lisa Lisa Lisa

> Hi Zach. Hope ur well. I can't chat til after election. Too overwhelemed w multiple issues.

We're all victims here. We need eachother to get through it. Don't isolate.

I love you 🌹

About the Author

Lisa La Bonté is a technology investor, global emerging markets expert and business advisor who has designed and delivered programs of impact related to emotional intelligence, innovation, STEM and/or millennial workforce and economic development for foreign monarchies, The World Bank, Department of Commerce, NASA, and under Executive Order of The White House as a U.S. Dept. of Defense Contractor. Lisa holds a B.A. in Political Science and an M.B.A. in International Business. Lisa has lived in Dubai for the past decade, yet having returned to USA just in time to be thrust into the sheer lunacy of the 2016 election cycle. The creation of this book has been cathartic!

Follow Lisa on Twitter: **@labontelisa**
& the Book **@ElectionDTox**

Remember to fuel the trend to relieve election stress by using **#WTFnov8**

Contact Lisa **info@WTFnov8.com**